THERE IS NO FEAR

KENNETH COPELAND

KENNETH
COPELAND
PUBLICATIONS

Unless otherwise indicated, all scripture quotations are from the *King James Version* of the Bible.

In Love There Is No Fear
ISBN 1-57562-677-2   30-0064

07 06 05 04 03 02   6 5 4 3 2 1

Kenneth Copeland Publications
Fort Worth, Texas 76192-0001

For more information about Kenneth Copeland Ministries, call
1-800-600-7395 or visit www.kcm.org.

In Love

T H E R E I S

N O F E A R

In World War II, Nazi Germany launched a series of air raids against the city of London. During those bombings the residents of London would evacuate their homes and businesses and take cover in designated underground shelters.

On one particular night of bombings, a woman turned up missing from her neighborhood shelter. A few days later some of her neighbors saw her and asked if everything was all right.

"Everything's fine," she replied.

"Then why were you not in the shelter the other night?" they asked.

"It's smelly down there," she said, "and I don't like it."

"Aren't you afraid the bombs will get you?" her friends asked.

"Oh, no," she said confidently. "I read the scripture where it says my God neither slumbers nor sleeps. So I decided there was no use in us both being awake. I just prayed, 'Lord, I praise You, I thank You and I place myself in Your love—and I'm not going to that shelter anymore.'"

Now there's a believer with a revelation of God's love. And it was that revelation of love that allowed this woman to overcome fear and roll the care of her well-being over onto God.

As it turned out, just a few days later, enemy aircraft came through and bombed that neighborhood and leveled every house. Every house, that is, except for the woman who chose to remain in the comfort of her home...and in the comfort of God's love.

You'll Know When It's True Love

As God's beloved and anointed children, it's amazing that we have not taken greater advantage of our authority and security that lies in the love of God, as this woman in London did.

Instead, through our ignorance and man-made, religious doctrines, we've allowed the devil to oppress us and keep us in all kinds of bondage. And all because of fear.

You may be wondering what possible connection there is between

God's love for you and having no fear. That connection is found in 1 John 4:

> Whosoever shall confess that Jesus is the Son of God, God dwelleth in him, and he in God. And we have known and believed the love that God hath to us. God is love: and he that dwelleth in love dwelleth in God, and God in him. Herein is our love made perfect, that we may have boldness in the day of judgment: because as he is, so are we in this world. There is no fear in love; but perfect love casteth out fear..." (verses 15-18).

God is Love. And *in* love, there is no fear. Not an ounce.

What's more, that love—which

leaves no room for fear—dwells in us. So neither should there be any fear in us. After all, we've not been given a spirit of fear, *"but of power, and of love..."* (2 Timothy 1:7).

> *God is Love. And in love, there is no fear. Not an ounce.*

For fear to enter into the heart of a believer, it must come from the outside, from the fear-infested world in which we live. And that's where *knowing* and *believing* the love of God comes into play for us.

Just moments before Jesus went to the cross, He prayed specifically for us:

> That they [we] may be made perfect in one; and that the world may know that thou hast sent me, and hast loved

them [us], as thou hast loved me....And I have declared unto them thy name, and will declare it: that the love where-with thou hast loved me may be in them, and I in them (John 17:23, 26).

The reason Jesus gave up His place in glory, came to earth, took on the limitations of human flesh, then went to the cross and suffered and died, was so He could make that transaction: *"that the love wherewith You [God] loved Me [Jesus] may be in them [us]."*

God loves us with the same love that He loves Jesus. And if He loves us to that degree, then He will certainly protect us to that degree. But we have to know and believe His love.

You knew the love of God the

moment you were born again. It was, in fact, love that recreated you. It was love that delivered you from the power of darkness, and translated you into the kingdom of His dear Son or "the Son of His love" as it literally translates (Colossians 1:13).

But how well do you know that love?

"Well I know God loves me, Brother Copeland. But I wouldn't go so far as to say He loves me just like He loves Jesus."

Then you're not walking in His love by faith. You're falling back on what your flesh—and probably the devil—is telling you.

The times you don't *feel* God's presence or *feel* God's love, those are the very times you had better believe He's there and believe His love for you. Otherwise, your flesh will let you down. Your mind will let you down. And Satan will use everything he can to pressure and push you away from the love of God.

I don't care how "spiritually dry" you might *feel*. That doesn't change a thing. The Word says the same thing today as it said yesterday. And it says, "In the beginning was the Word, and the Word was with God, and the Word was God" (John 1:1).

The Word is God. And God is Love. So the Word is Love.

Get up every day determined to let only the Word—Love—tell you what you *feel*—not your flesh, not your circumstances and certainly not the devil. Listen to love tell you, *"I will never leave thee, nor forsake thee"* (Hebrews 13:5).

Remember, when we have known and believed the love of God, *"herein is our love made perfect"* (1 John 4:17).

The Perfect Love Story

Another aspect of our love being perfected is found in 1 John 2:4-5: *"He that saith, I know him [I know God, I know Jesus, I know love], and keepeth not his [God's] commandments, is a liar, and the truth is not in him. But whoso keepeth his [God's] word, in him verily is the love of God perfected."*

When you keep God's Word, you allow the love of God to run its full course in your life. You reach that place of allowing God to do what He designed Himself to do on the inside of you. It's what God had in mind when He created Adam. It's what He was in Jesus. And that's exactly what He plans to be in you.

But notice that the key to being perfected in God's love is tied to keeping His commandments—His

Word. First John 3:23 says: "And this is his [God's] commandment, That we should believe on the name of his Son Jesus Christ, and love one another, as he gave us commandment."

This verse refers to the commandment Jesus gave to His disciples: "A new commandment I give unto you, That ye love one another; as I have loved you..." (John 13:34).

Love one another as I have loved you...

"We can't do that, Jesus!"

Of course we can't. That's why 1 John 3:23 precedes the commandment to love with "Believe on the name of his Son Jesus Christ...." Then we can love one another.

That changes the complexion of this thing. It takes love out of the emotional realm and puts it in the spiritual realm. In other words, it's going to take believing on the Name of Jesus the Anointed One to be able to love one another the way He did. It's going to take faith.

Also realize from these two passages that we're talking about a commandment from Jesus. If He commanded us to love, then somehow He must have equipped us to do it.

Besides, Jesus did not love us with some human form of love. He loved us with the love of God—and that's not just any love.

> *If Jesus commanded us to love, then somehow He must have equipped us to do it.*

Throughout His earthly ministry, Jesus used a Greek word for *love* that was as uncommon as He was. It's the word we know as *agape*.

The people of Jesus' day didn't

really understand the word because it was not a word used in conversation. It was primarily used in classic writings and so forth.

We find *agape* used in the writings of the Apostle Paul, particularly in that great passage on love, 1 Corinthians 13. But even the English translators translated love as *charity,* which is closer to the true meaning because charity is more than just love.

Charity is actually a love that has a driving desire to give. So agape, as used by Jesus, is more than just loving one another. It is loving one another to the point that you are willing to give yourself.

"I Do..."

In John 21:15-17, Jesus asked Peter three times, "Do you love Me?" or "Do you agape Me?" Peter had to answer three times before he got it right because he was trying to answer Jesus in the language of the day. He just didn't understand what Jesus was saying.

Agape is the key to the command to love. It's the key to loving as Jesus loved.

To get the love of God—the *agape* kind of love—over to mankind, Jesus entered into a blood covenant with God. With the sacrifice of His own blood, Jesus said, "I agape!"

To *agape* is an act of the will. It is a spoken covenant from which there is no retreat, and about which there is no debate.

So you can get in it and receive it by partaking of His covenant, or you can stay on the outside of it and go straight to hell. Either way, God will love you all the way there because the covenant has been made. He said, *I love!* And that was that.

> *Jesus used His will to love. And you must use your will to receive.*

Jesus used His will to love. And you must use your will to receive.

But without the help of God, we don't have the natural ability to love unconditionally. And He doesn't expect us to keep the commandment to love by our flesh, our natural man. That's where the old covenant was a problem. The children of Israel demonstrated just how weak this flesh really is.

Today, however, we have the blood of Jesus, we have His Name that is above every name and we have the Spirit of Almighty God dwelling inside us. That's Love Himself living in us. All we have to do is make the decision to keep the commandment. God will take care of the rest.

But if we don't commit to the commandment to love, we face the consequences in 1 John 2:10-11: "He that loveth his brother abideth in the light, and there is none occasion of stumbling in him. But he that hateth his brother is in darkness, and walketh in darkness, and knoweth not whither he goeth, because that darkness hath blinded his eyes."

Come Out of the Dark

Pure and simple...hate is strife. But our idea of hate is that surge of emotion—*rage*—just before you decide whether or not to do serious damage to someone because you're angry with them. But not so.

When Adam was changed from life to death, his faith turned into fear. And the love of God inside him turned into hate because he was now connected to Satan.

Yes, there are different degrees of hate, but it's still all hate. And the slightest bit of it is just as mean and dangerous as the highest degree of it.

You may not be out to kill someone, but you're killing yourself. Because that's what hate will do. It will kill you, it will age you and it will ruin your day.

I'm talking about all those little

hate-full things someone might think, say or do, all day long, never realizing what's actually happening. It's that strife that builds and builds—all day long, all week long, your whole life long.

That's where you need to repent and deal with those things the moment they pop up. Don't even allow the smallest grain of hate—or strife—to remain in your spirit. Because, keep in mind, we're dealing with fear here. We're dealing with the spiritual connection to death (Hebrews 2:14-15).

So walking around with hatred in your heart toward your brother is not going to perfect the love of God in your life. The love that in turn casts out all fear.

No, 1 John 2:11 says strife will throw you out in the dark.

And what's out in the dark? Fear.

The moment fear presents itself to you in any shape or form, realize that you don't have a fear problem. Your problem is in fulfilling the commandment to love as Jesus loved.

Maybe you shot your mouth off at someone when you shouldn't have. Or are you holding on to something that someone said or did that hurt you, and you have not—or you've refused to—forgive them.

The point is, get before God and judge yourself. Ask Him to reveal the problem and take the time to deal with it...immediately.

Then commit to the love walk. That means loving the person you have problems with—oftentimes, by faith.

As you do, the love of God will be perfected in you. And all fear will be cast out. Then it won't be long until you'll be falling in love.

The love that never leaves you, nor forsakes you. It casts out all fear and never leaves you in the dark. It's the love that never fails.

Prayer for Salvation and Baptism in the Holy Spirit

Heavenly Father, I come to You in the Name of Jesus. Your Word says, "Whosoever shall call on the name of the Lord shall be saved" (Acts 2:21). I am calling on You. I pray and ask Jesus to come into my heart and be Lord over my life according to Romans 10:9-10. "If thou shalt confess with thy mouth the Lord Jesus, and shalt believe in thine heart that God hath raised him from the dead, thou shalt be saved. For with the heart man believeth unto righteousness; and with the mouth confession is made unto salvation." I do that now. I confess that Jesus is Lord, and I believe in my heart that God raised Him from the dead.

I am now reborn! I am a Christian— a child of Almighty God! I am saved! You also said in Your Word, "If ye then, being evil, know how to give good gifts unto your children: HOW MUCH MORE shall your heavenly Father give the Holy Spirit to them that ask him?" (Luke 11:13). I'm also asking You to fill me with the Holy Spirit.

Holy Spirit, rise up within me as I praise God. I fully expect to speak with other tongues as You give me the utterance (Acts 2:4). In Jesus' Name. Amen!

Begin to praise God for filling you with the Holy Spirit. Speak those words and syllables you receive—not in your own language, but the language given to you by the Holy Spirit. You have to use your own voice. God will not force you to speak. Don't be concerned with how it sounds. It is a heavenly language!

Continue with the blessing God has given you and pray in the spirit every day.

You are a born-again, Spirit-filled believer. You'll never be the same!

Find a good Word of God preaching church, and become a part of a church family who will love and care for you as you love and care for them.

We need to be connected to each other. It increases our strength in God. It's God's plan for us.

About the Author

Kenneth Copeland is co-founder and president of Kenneth Copeland Ministries in Fort Worth, Texas, and best-selling author of books that include *Managing God's Mutual Funds—Yours and His, How to Discipline Your Flesh* and *Honor—Walking in Honesty, Truth and Integrity.*

Now in his 35th year as minister of the gospel of Christ and teacher of God's Word, Kenneth is the recording artist of such award-winning albums as his Grammy nominated *Only the Redeemed, In His Presence, He Is Jehovah* and his most recently released *Just a Closer Walk.* He also co-stars as the character Wichita Slim in the children's adventure videos *The Gunslinger, Covenant Rider* and the movie *The Treasure of Eagle Mountain,* and as Daniel Lyon in the *Commander Kellie and the Superkids*_{SM} videos *Armor of Light* and *Judgment: The Trial of Commander Kellie.*

With the help of offices and staff in the United States, Canada, England, Australia, South Africa and Ukraine, Kenneth is fulfilling his vision to boldly preach the uncompromised Word of God from the top of this world, to the bottom, and all the way around. His ministry reaches millions of people worldwide through daily and Sunday TV broadcasts, magazines, teaching tapes and videos, conventions and campaigns, and the World Wide Web.

Learn more about
Kenneth Copeland Ministries
by visiting our Web site at
www.kcm.org.

Books Available From
Kenneth Copeland Ministries

by Kenneth Copeland

*   A Ceremony of Marriage
     A Matter of Choice
     Covenant of Blood
     Faith and Patience—The Power Twins
*   Freedom From Fear
     Giving and Receiving
     Honor—Walking in Honesty, Truth and Integrity
     How to Conquer Strife
     How to Discipline Your Flesh
     How to Receive Communion
     In Love There Is No Fear
     Know Your Enemy
     Living at the End of Time—A Time of Supernatural Increase
     Love Never Fails
     Managing God's Mutual Funds—Yours and His
     Mercy—The Divine Rescue of the Human Race
*   Now Are We in Christ Jesus
     One Nation Under God (gift book with CD enclosed)
*   Our Covenant With God
     Partnership, Sharing the Vision—Sharing the Grace
*   Prayer—Your Foundation for Success
*   Prosperity: The Choice Is Yours
     Rumors of War
*   Sensitivity of Heart
*   Six Steps to Excellence in Ministry
*   Sorrow Not! Winning Over Grief and Sorrow
*   The Decision Is Yours
*   The Force of Faith
*   The Force of Righteousness
     The Image of God in You
     The Laws of Prosperity

The Grace That Makes Us Holy
The Power to Live a New Life
The Protection of Angels
The Unbeatable Spirit of Faith
* Walk in the Spirit (Available in Spanish only)
Walk With God
Well Worth the Wait
Words That Heal (gift book and CD enclosed)
Your Promise of Protection—The Power of the 91st Psalm

Books Co-Authored by Kenneth and Gloria Copeland

Family Promises
Healing Promises
Prosperity Promises
Protection Promises

* From Faith to Faith—A Daily Guide to Victory
From Faith to Faith—A Perpetual Calendar

One Word From God Series

- One Word From God Can Change Your Destiny
- One Word From God Can Change Your Family
- One Word From God Can Change Your Finances
- One Word From God Can Change Your Formula for Success
- One Word From God Can Change Your Health
- One Word From God Can Change Your Nation
- One Word From God Can Change Your Prayer Life
- One Word From God Can Change Your Relationships

Over The Edge—A Youth Devotional
Pursuit of His Presence—A Daily Devotional
Pursuit of His Presence—A Perpetual Calendar

Other Books Published by KCP

The First 30 Years—A Journey of Faith
    The story of the lives of Kenneth and Gloria Copeland.

Real People. Real Needs. Real Victories.

A book of testimonies to encourage your faith.

John G. Lake—His Life, His Sermons, His Boldness of Faith

The Holiest of All by Andrew Murray

The New Testament in Modern Speech by
Richard Francis Weymouth

Unchained by Mac Gober

Products Designed for Today's Children and Youth

And Jesus Healed Them All (confession book and CD gift package)

Baby Praise Board Book

Baby Praise Christmas Board Book

Noah's Ark Coloring Book

The Best of *Shout!* Adventure Comics

The *Shout!* Giant Flip Coloring Book

The *Shout!* Joke Book

The *Shout!* Super-Activity Book

Wichita Slim's Campfire Stories

*Commander Kellie and the Superkids*_{SM} *Books:*

The SWORD Adventure Book

*Commander Kellie and the Superkids*_{SM} Solve-It-
Yourself Mysteries

*Commander Kellie and the Superkids*_{SM} Adventure Series
Middle Grade Novels by Christopher P.N. Maselli

#1 The Mysterious Presence

#2 The Quest for the Second Half

#3 Escape From Jungle Island

#4 In Pursuit of the Enemy

#5 Caged Rivalry

#6 Mystery of the Missing Junk

#7 Out of Breath

#8 The Year Mashela Stole Christmas

*Available in Spanish

World Offices of
Kenneth Copeland Ministries

For more information about KCM and a free
catalog, please write the office nearest you:

Kenneth Copeland Ministries
Fort Worth, Texas 76192-0001

Kenneth Copeland
Locked Bag 2600
Mansfield Delivery Centre
QUEENSLAND 4122
AUSTRALIA

Kenneth Copeland
Post Office Box 15
BATH
BA1 3XN
ENGLAND U.K.

Kenneth Copeland
Private Bag X 909
FONTAINEBLEAU
2032
REPUBLIC OF
SOUTH AFRICA

Kenneth Copeland
Post Office Box 378
Surrey, B.C.
V3T 5B6
CANADA

Kenneth Copeland Ministries
Post Office Box 84
L'VIV 79000
UKRAINE

We're Here for You!

Believer's Voice of Victory
Television Broadcast

Join Kenneth and Gloria Copeland and the *Believer's Voice of Victory* broadcasts Monday through Friday and on Sunday each week, and learn how faith in God's Word can take your life from ordinary to extraordinary. This teaching from God's Word is designed to get you where you want to be—*on top!*

You can catch the *Believer's Voice of Victory* broadcast on your local, cable or satellite channels.

*Check your local listings for times and stations in your area.

Believer's Voice of Victory Magazine

Enjoy inspired teaching and encouragement from Kenneth and Gloria Copeland and guest ministers each month in the *Believer's Voice of Victory* magazine. Also included are real-life testimonies of God's miraculous power and divine intervention in the lives of people just like you!

It's more than just a magazine—it's a ministry.

Shout! The Voice of Victory for Kids

Shout!...The dynamic magazine just for kids is a Bible-charged, action-packed, bimonthly magazine available FREE to kids everywhere! Featuring Wichita Slim and *Commander Kellie and the Superkids*_{SM}, *Shout!* is filled with colorful adventure comics, challenging games and puzzles, exciting short stories, solve-it-yourself mysteries and much more!!

Stand up, sign up and get ready to *Shout!*

To receive a FREE subscription to *Believer's Voice of Victory,* or to give a child you know a FREE subscription to *Shout!,* write:

Kenneth Copeland Ministries
Fort Worth, Texas 76192-0001

Or call: 1-800-600-7395   (9 a.m.-5 p.m. CT)
Or visit our Web site at: www.kcm.org

If you are writing from outside the U.S., please contact the KCM office nearest you. Addresses for all Kenneth Copeland Ministries offices are listed on the previous pages.

KENNETH COPELAND MINISTRIES